A New Ap

Jürgen Buschmann/Hubertus Bussmann/Klaus Pabst

COORDINATION –
A NEW APPROACH TO SOCCER COACHING

Soccer Training in Game Form for Children & Young People

Meyer & Meyer Sport

Original Title: Koordination-das neue Fußballtraining
Aachen: Meyer und Meyer, 2000
Translated by Robert McMurray

British Library Cataloguing in Publication Data
A catalogue record for this book is available from the British Library

Buschmann/Pabst/Bussmann:
Coordination-a New Approach to Soccer Coaching/Jürgen Buschmann;
Klaus Pabst; Hubertus Bussmann
Oxford: Meyer & Meyer Sport (UK) Ltd., 2002
ISBN 1-84126-063-0

© 2002 by Meyer & Meyer Sport (UK) Ltd.
Aachen, Adelaide, Auckland, Budapest, Graz, Johannesburg,
Miami, Olten (CH), Oxford, Singapore, Toronto
Member of the World
 Sports Publishers' Association
www.w-s-p-a.org

Printed and bound in Germany
by: Druckpunkt, Bergheim
ISBN 1-84126-063-0
E-Mail: verlag@meyer-meyer-sports.com
www.meyer-meyer-sports.com

CONTENTS

Contents

Throughout this book, the pronouns he, she, him, her and so on are interchangeable and intended to be inclusive of both men and women. It is important in sport, as elsewhere, that men and women have equal status and opportunities.

Introduction

The importance of coordination for the soccer player has become a greater point of interest over the last few years and always is a popular subject of discussion. This is especially because it does not seem to be by chance that the successful European soccer-playing countries, in particular e.g. the relatively small Netherlands or France, the winner of the 1998 World Championship, attach greatest importance to the best possible training in coordination and technique.

In these countries a daily one-hour training session in coordination has been a matter of course for years. In this connection the Ajax Soccer School in Amsterdam is especially famous. But also in France, talented players in soccer boarding schools, which are compulsory for professional clubs, receive special support of this nature.

Only those players best able to control their bodies and the ball are capable of top performance in soccer. In spite of all their various and individual requirements top players have and had one thing in common, i.e. they are able to control their bodies and the ball in almost all situations during the game.

A best possible development of coordination undoubtedly leads to increased performance in playing soccer and results in increased learning ability. This can only develop best when taught in good time – it cannot take place "too early", but only "too late". This requires the best coaches available who have been well trained and who have sufficient teaching experience, rather than short-term "success coaches".

The example set by the coach is never more important than for children. But attractive, soccer-related coordination training is essential not just for the youngest players. With a little patience and sensitivity even shortcomings in coordination in Junior As and Junior Bs as well as for Seniors can be corrected.

In coordination training complex movement models, rather than certain movements (technique), are taught. The cultivation of these coordinative abilities form the basis on which technically simple and complex demands can be more easily learned and executed. The games and exercises described in this book were intentionally taken from technical elements of soccer playing so that they can be used by those coaches not so conversant with coordination coaching. Of course

we are well aware that many exercises and types of games teach not only those techniques that they are supposed to teach, but also can have the effect of being general or fundamental or/and compensatory. In this way both beginners as well as specialists in coodination training will find many ideas for coaching.

Jürgen Buschmann
Hubertus Bussmann
Klaus Pabst

Cologne, 19 August 1999

1 THE BASICS OF COORDINATION TRAINING

Coordination is the basics and a requirement for every movement of our daily motor activity. This is especially true in a sports context. The better the quality of coordination, the higher the related performance with a simultaneous saving in the amount of energy involved.

Besides strength, speed, endurance and flexibility, coordination comprises the fifth area of the physical abilities. All areas depend on each other and exert a considerable influence on the soccer player's ability to move and perform on the field (c.f. Diagram 1). Till now this special aspect of soccer training has been given too little or consciously and systematically even no emphasis.

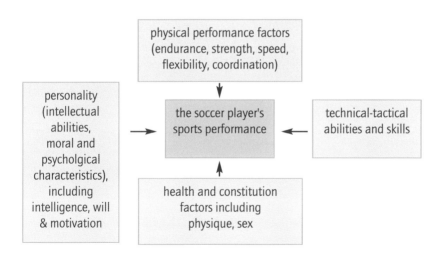

Diagram 1: Elements of sports performance ability

Definition: Coordination means the interaction of the central nervous system (CNS) and the skeletal muscles during a given movement.

THE BASICS

A distinction is made between:
a) intramuscular coordination
   * coordination of individual muscle fibres within a muscle.
b) intermuscular coordination
   * coordination of all muscles with each other.

Coordination training, and hence technique training, begins not only at young peoples' F-Grade level in soccer but at birth. Multi-faceted "training" i.e. with the hands, legs, feet, torso and corresponding equipment, is the basis for good fundamental training in soccer. These days, where movement and movement games are not necessarily part of the natural environment of childrens' lives – if there is no playground around the corner for example – more and more, we find children with underdeveloped motor skills. This is also the case with coordination (c.f. Table I), and of course in soccer itself.

* Bad aiming accuracy e.g when passing or shooting.
* Loss of spatial orientation e.g. when a player in defence positions himself against an opponent.
* The inability to adapt to a partner or a piece of training equipment, e.g when offering oneself, getting into space or judging the flight of the ball.
* Awkward, abrupt or arythmic movements, e.g. when running with or without the ball.
* Superfluous movement within a complex movement, e.g. "rowing" with the arms when running.
* Catching objects in an inflexible manner e.g. when acting as a goalkeeper.
* Landing awkwardly on the ground, e.g. after heading the ball.
* Unsteadiness on a smaller base of support e.g. standing on one leg.

Table 1: Possible weak points in coordination in soccer players

Basics: Each child is born with between 160 and 180 thousand million nerve cells in his brain, which reduce to 100 thousand million by about ten years of age. Initially the cells are not connected. The more of these connections are developed (synapses), the better the intellectual abilities become in later life. The most effective means of preserving the cells and building up the synapses is movement in the coordinative sense. This is why play-like activities – especially ball-games – are extremely important for the personality development.

However there is a minor problem premature in special training, e.g. as a soccer player: no one sport trains all coordinative abilities equally well. This is why children especially need so-called complementary sports training in order to ensure an as widely based, varied coordination training as possible, including elements from field athletics, gymnastics and dancing.

Elements of coordinative ability: Complex coordinative ability in soccer can be divided into the following subgroups:

Coordination abilities	Examples in soccer	Games and practice leading to improved coordination
Ability of adaptation and adjustment		
the ability to adjust to unexpected and new situations as quickly as possible	e.g. bouncing of the ball in various weather and field conditions	types of games and exercises on various field conditions / with different balls (e.g. beach soccer, indoor, hard surface or grass field, on snow or during heavy rain)
Anticipation ability		
the ability to anticipate the results and order of the actions and reactions of other players	anticipating the actions of the team mates or opponents	complex forms of playing, best competitive game itself
Ability of differentiation		
the ability to use the muscles sensitively and consciously controlled (precise and economic movement)	e.g. playing headers when jumping (requires use of strength for jumping up and heading the ball), the goalkeeper's "Jump for a high ball"	- functional exercises - exercises with varying uses of strength (e.g. goal-shot: hard, mid-strength, low - with spin)

	(use of strength when jumping to get exactly the necessary height), "feeling for the ball"	- stopping and controlling the ball
Peripheral vision ability		
ability to orientate one-self by means of spatial perception and to act accordingly	noticing team-mates and or opponents and the ball and have them in one's sight. This is a requirement for useful tactical action.	- technique exercises in which an extra task must be carried out at a sign from the coach - complex games (with breaks from the coach in which he points out mistakes)
Timing ability		
the ability to carry out a movement at exactly the right moment	coordinating of the ball path in the air with one's own movement e.g. jumping up for a header after a cross	technique ball exercises including use of various crosses (from various positions and with varying height and force) by head and feet
Balance ability		
ability to maintain balance or to restore it as quickly as possible	e.g. after tackling with body contact	- tackling exercises - running exercises with extra tasks e.g. rolling and turning
Ability to combine partial movements		
the ability to combine partial movements with each other into a flowing and economic whole movement	e.g. "Headers" (jumping up, getting the body ready, head the ball); "the goalkepper's kickout" (arm and body movement).	lining up of various technique elements: stopping and controlling the ball and goal shot.

Orientation ability

the ability to determine the position of one's body in the space (e.g. on the playing field) or in relation to an object (e.g. the ball or other players)	e.g. "offering oneself and getting into space" (orienting oneself to the ball, to other players, spatially); when the goalie runs out of the goal (he has to orientate himself within the penalty area, to the ball and to the other players).	during technique exercises e.g. at a goal shot, add other movement exercises e.g. turns, rolls, or jumping over hurdles

Reaction ability

the ability to react appropriately in response to special stimuli as fast as possible	e.g. using fake kicks, reacting to feints, keeping shots from closest distance (goalkeeper) or reacting more quickly than an opponent	- a short running race after an acoustic or visual signal from the coach - games using several balls or various balls including a rugby ball; goalshot (stand with one's back to the coach, who then shouts and throws the ball. The player then turns and shoots).

Ability of adaptation to rhythm

the ability to get into one's own movement rhythm (tensing and relaxing of the working muscle groupes)	e.g. running up to shoot or head the ball, the stride rhythm of the goalie before jumping up for high balls, before diving for it or before a kickout of his hand	- carrying out deceptive movements - dribbling exercises along various slalom courses - frequent repeating of feints - ball control left and right in a rhythmic change

Partial abilities are closely and mutually interrelated, but can still develop independently from one another, just as they can be trained jointly and serverally. Of course these partial abilities are not all called for in the same manner in a soccer game . Balance, rhythm and differentiation abilities are certainly called on more in a sport such as gymnastics. In a soccer game the emphasis is on the improvement of reaction, orientation and anticipation abilities. Furthermore the peripheral vision ability is taught as well as the right timing of passes.

The objective of teaching coordination: Coordination is supposed to achieve the best results with regard to the best movement using as few muscles and as little tension as possible. In soccer the objective is a good and well-adapted mastery of body and ball in various situations. Coordination training is also good for learning new, soccer-related movement techniques more quickly.

With improved coodination the coach creates the prerequisites for improved technical skills in his players, especially technical creativity and variability.

As a result, one usually differentiates between good
* *general coordination,* or "agilty", and
* *specific coordination*, or " dexterity".
    - **agility** is a harmonious spacious succession of movements, "everyday motor skills" e.g. when running, jumping, diving or falling.
    - **dexterity** consists of harmonious limited actions and is related to a particular sport e.g. handling a ball: dribbling, juggling and ball control.

Training means: the exercises and games used in coordination training may consist of the soccer game itself on the one hand and other sports on the other (demand for general sports training).

The best age for learning: the pre-pubescent years and the first stage of early puberty (from about six to 14 years of age) is the best time for carrying out coordination exercises, but even in the pre-school years (up to six years) coordination demands on the body are especially important. Generally speaking the quality of coordination with children and young people increases steadily and peaks at between 18 and 20 years of age.

This means that, for coordination training in the various stages of development, especially in the Junior E and F grades, a broad basis of coordination skills must be developed (c.f. Table 2). From the age of puberty all coordination skills should then be developed further.

	Junior F (6-8 years)	Junior E (8-10 years)	Junior D (10-12 years)	Junior C (12-14 years)
Endurance			low	average
Agility	low	low	high	high
Coordination				
Adaptation/adjustment	high	high	average	average
Anticipation	high	high	average	average
Differentiation	high	high	average	average
Timing	high	high	average	average
Balance	average	average	low	low
Orientation	high	high	average	average
Reaction	high	high	average	average
Rhythm	average	average	low	low
Strength	low	low	average	average
Speed	high	high	average	average

Table 2: Training contents of physical abilities in the various stages of development (= high, = average, = low amount)

16

Methodical Principles: When training the following guidelines should be borne in mind:

- The players should only train when not being tired, i.e. after the warm-up.
- All exercises and games should be carried out as fast as each individual player is capable of.
- The loading time of each exercise should not exceed a period of 20 to 30 seconds.
- The number of repetitions depends on the degree of the most efficient way of carrying out each movement, i.e. when a player has mastered a particular exercise, change it! Train initially under simplified, then increasingly more difficult, conditions: pressure of time and from opponents must be constantly increased.
- Vary the way of movement sequences (c.f. Table 3).

 Variation of movement perfomance
- altering the area the ball is aimed at and the way the players shoot the ball:
  - flat/high/in the middle/corner of the goal
  - kicking with the inner/front/outer instep
- variation of strength tension:
  - low/medium/heavy
  - lob/powerful shot

 Variation of exercise conditions
- variation of balls and angles of shot:
  - light/heavy, large/ small balls
  - 11 m/16 m/20 m
  - acute/open angle
- altering the starting position
  - ball at rest or in motion
  - after dribbling, cross, stopping the ball
  - fast or slow (limited time period)
  - with or without an opponent (active/passive)
  - using both feet (right, left)

and so on.

Table 3: Variation of movement performance

- Exercises should be carried out precisely, quickly and rhythmically.
- Combine exercises and game forms with each other.

- Coordinative-technical training should always be accompanied by corresponding training in agility. This creates a high level of flexibility in the joints and muscular elasticity.
- Use exercises which are as different as possible i.e. create individual success experiences.
- Every now and then the various exercises and game forms can be carried out at the end of the training session (the objective is to increase the concentration when being tired).

Tips for the coach: When carrying out coordination exercises and game forms, the following points should be borne in mind:

- Create a positive atmosphere: training should be "fun".

- The players should nevertheless be challenged, motivated and get to concentrate on the game.

- Ensure that movements are carried out precisely.

- Keep correcting mistakes.

- Pay attention to an optimal individual level of demand – let every player succeed at his own level.

- Focus the training on the players; encourage creativity by letting them discover training variations of their own.

- Get the players to practise also at home: set "homework" such as juggling, catching, throwing etc.

2 COORDINATION TRAINING IN PRACTICE

A)   Main Focus: Technique

Simply characterised, a football player's performance is made up of four basic elements or components:
- physical ability
- tactical performance ability
- technical skills
- psychological abilities

The level of the single basic elements determines a player's playing ability. Only when a player has acquired abilities, skills and knowledge in all four areas he is capable of acting according to the objective of the game. The higher a player's ability in the single basic elements can be assessed, the higher his level of playing ability will be. In the following two chapters two of the four basic elements of soccer will be looked at separately, firstly technique and then tactics.

> Technique describes the ideal model of a movement and the putting of this "ideal movement" into practice (GROSSER/NEUMAIER 1982). "Technique in a soccer game describes all the movements selected according to the rules to solve a particular task" (KOLLATH 1991).

Technique in soccer consists of three areas:

Movements without the ball
standing, walking, trotting, running, sprinting

Movements towards the ball
jumping, pushing, tackling

Movements with the ball	
dribbling/feinting	passing
goal shot	ball control
heading the ball	acting as goalkeeper

In the following chapters forms of coordinative exercises and game forms for soccer-related movements with the ball will be described. A short definition of each technique (e.g. "What is passing?") is preceded by a description of various ways in which it may be applied in a game (e.g. "Where does passing take place in a game?"), and a large number of various techniques (e.g. "How are passes performed?").

1   Dribbling/Feinting

Dribbling and feinting techniques present elementary, basic technical skills, since they are considered to be the basis for a vast number of more advanced soccer techniques.

While at the upper end of the performance scale, dribbling as a dominant technique may tend to be relegated more and more to the background (in favour of a rapid moving game), it will still in future remain absolutely essential to equip soccer players with these indispensible tools, of which dribbling is the most important.

There are three different types of **dribbling**:

- Dribbling while keeping the ball

  Dribbling while keeping the ball is carried out mainly with the instep. It is used to ensure possession of the ball within the player's own team. The ball remains under control without gaining any significant ground into the direction of the opponents' goal. This type of dribbling is used when the speed of the game is to be reduced or while the player with the ball is waiting for support from his team mates.

- Fast dribbling

  Fast dribbling, also known as dribbling to gain distance, takes place at high or top speed. Because of the high speed the ball is dribbled mainly with the instep. Fast dribbling can be carried out in a controlled manner and the player can cover large distances on the field, as for example after intercepting an opposing attack immediately followed by an own counterattack.

- Dribbling with feints

  Dribbling with feints is performed mainly with the inner and outer edges and the sole of the foot. When dribbling and feinting the player is directly confronted by at least one opponent whom he tries to outplay. When a player dribbles and feints he can use countless individual techniques: dribbling at various speeds (varying-speed feints), body feints, walking feints, shooting and passing feints, as well as feinting by changing direction or just by looking in the wrong direction.

- Body/Walking feints

  By transferring the direction of his torso or walking a few paces a player can fake going in a certain direction and, depending on the reaction from his opponent, continue his path in the other direction (also known as the Mathews-Trick, the double/simple/outside/inside step over, the Beckenbauer turn, the Locomotive/Leo or the sole trick).

- Shooting and passing feints

  The player with the ball pretends to shoot or pass the ball and then, after his opponent has reacted (standing leg) dribbles it past him.

- "Change-of direction" feints

  While running with the ball the player changes direction at irregular intervals.

- "Varying-speed"-feints

  The player with the ball slows down briefly in order to suddenly accelerate past his opponent.

- Feinting by looking in the wrong direction

  The player with the ball tricks his opponent by looking in one direction and then he starts in the other one.

Tips on carrying out feints

- Get the eye away from the ball and look about three metres in front of the ball on the ground (the ball, other team members and opponents in the peripheral field of vision).

- Closed dribbling, that means, the player should touch the ball as often as possible (with the leading foot at every step forward).

- The player's body must be interposed between the ball and the opponent so that the ball can be shielded.

- The feints must be used deliberately. If the player's opponent reacts to a feint, the player must outplay him with a quick kick to the side of the standing leg.

Training Forms for Dribbling and Feinting

a) Running around Poles/Dribbling

Equipment

Eight poles, four cones and a ball for each player.

Preparation

Three metres in front of two start cones, standing side by side (three metres apart), four poles are putting across in a row (pole distance 0,5m). Another cone stands outside each row of poles about 1.5 metres apart. The coach positions himself as a return position in the centre of the field four metres behind the poles. The players line up in two groups at each start cone.

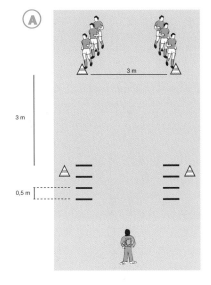

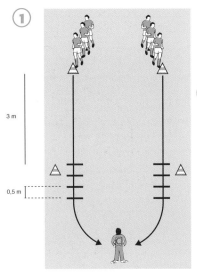

Procedure

Exercises without ball

Exercise 1:

At a sign from the coach (acoustic/visual) the first player of each group runs over the poles to the coach and claps at him. At every gap between the poles each player must touch the ground with one foot.

Exercise 2:

As in Exercise 1, except that the players no longer run in a straight line past the poles but from the start diagonally to the side and over their opponents' poles to the coach (changing sides, orientation).

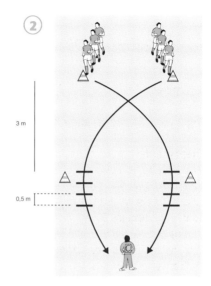

Exercise 3:

The players run around the poles on their side once and then in a straight line to the coach.

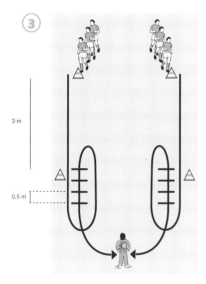

Exercise 4:

As in Exercise 3, except that the players now run around the other side's poles and then over them to the coach (changing sides, orientation).

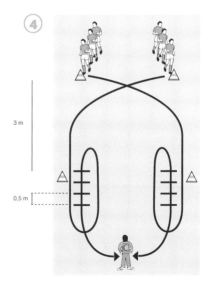

Exercise 5:

The players run in slalom fashion around the poles to the coach.

Exercise 6:

As in Exercise 5, except that the players run in slalom fashion over the other side's poles to the coach (changing sides, orientation).

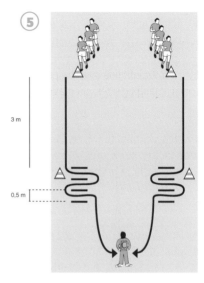

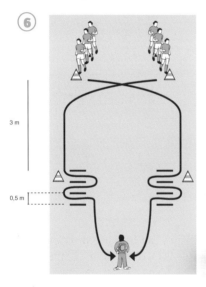

Exercise 7:

As in Exercises 1-6, except that there are now gaps of varying distances between the poles.

Exercise 8:

As in Exercises 1-7, except that the coach increases or reduces the distance at which he is standing away from the poles, thus altering the running distance.

Exercises with the ball

Exercise 9:

The players now dribble the ball once around the poles, place it at the outer cone and then run in a straight line over the poles to the coach.

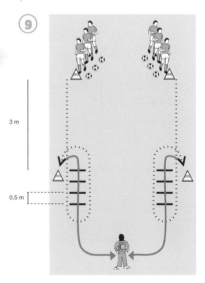

Exercise 10:

As in Exercise 9, except that the players now dribble the ball around the other group's poles, put it down at the cone and run in a straight line over the poles to the coach (changing sides, orientation).

Exercise 11:

The players dribble the ball in a slalom around the posts, put it down at the cone and run in a straight line over the poles to the coach.

Exercise 12:

As in Exercise 11, except that the players now dribble the ball around the other team's poles, put it down at the cone and run over the poles to the coach (changing sides, orientation).

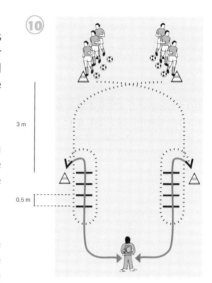

Tips for the coach

- More variations of exercises and game forms can be made by changing the directions the players have to run or to dribble (or combinations of these).
- Include variations to the starts: turns, jumps, doing a roll at starting.
- Let the players perform exercises as a competition: "Who can be the first to clap at the coach?

b) Dribbling around Cones

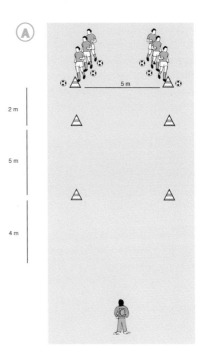

Equipment

Six cones and one ball per player.

Preparation

Two metres in front of two start cones placed side by side (about five metres apart), four other cones mark a dribbling area 5 m in length. The coach stands four metres behind the dribbling area as return position. The players stand in two groups of the same number at the starting cones.

Procedure

Exercise 1:

The first player in each group dribbles the ball in a circuit right around the two cones in front of their starting point. At an acoustic or visual sign from the coach the players leave the ball down and sprint to the coach and clap at him.

32

Exercise 2:

As in Exercise 1, except that the players now dribble the ball diagonally around the cones so that they constantly cross each other (orientation to the ball and to the opponents).

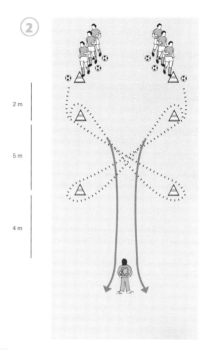

Exercise 3:

As Exercise 1, except that the players now dribble the ball around all four cones in the dribbling area. One player dribbles from the right, the other one from the left. In this way the players meet each other regularly while dribbling (orientation to the ball and to the opponents).

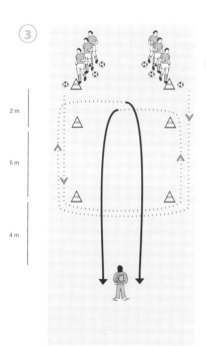

Tips for the coach

* Other variations of exercises/game forms can be made with extra tasks at signs from the coach (e.g. turns, jumps, rolls).
* Exercises and game-forms can be carried out as competitions: "Who can clap at the coach first?"

c) Slalom Running/Slalom Dribbling

Equipment

Eight slalom poles, two cones and one ball per player.

Preparation

Two starting cones stand three metres apart from each other. Two metres in front of every cone, a slalom course is set by four slalom poles for each team (1,5 m distance between). The players line up in two evenly-numbered teams at each starting cone.

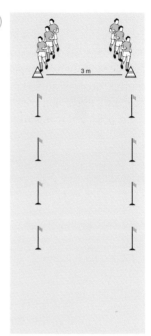

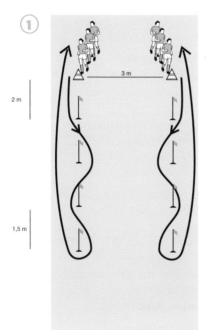

Procedure

Exercises without the ball –
Slalom running

Exercise 1:
The players run the slalom course and return around the outside to the starting point.

Exercise 2:
The players run the slalom course but then, at a sign from the coach (acoustic/visual) add various movements to the run: a turn > continue the slalom, a jump > continue the slalom, a roll > continue the slalom. The players return to the starting point along the outside of the poles.

Exercise 3:

As in Exercise 1, except the players now do not run back along the outside. Instead they run back through the other team's slalom course, so that they finish at the other starting cone (orientation to the poles and to a partner).

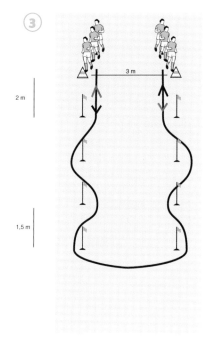

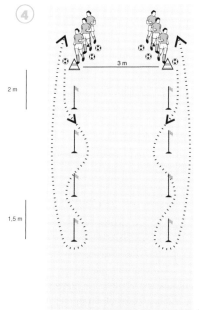

Exercises with the ball – Slalom dribbling

Exercise 4:

The players dribble the ball through the slalom course and then back along the outside to the starting point.

Exercise 5:

The players dribble the ball through the slalom course and then, at a sign from the coach (acoustic/visual), they dribble the ball all the way around the nearest slalom pole. Then they continue dribbling the ball through the course and along the outside back to the starting point.

35

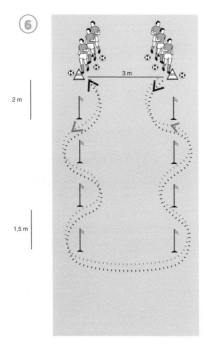

Exercise 6:

As in Exercise 4, except that the players now do not run back along the outside. Instead they dribble the ball back through the other team's slalom course as well (orientation to the poles, to the ball and to a partner).

Tips for the coach

• All exercises and game-forms can be varied in a way that the players change sides immediately after the start and run or dribble through the other team's slalom course.

• Teaching vision skills: when running or dribbling around the poles each player should pay attention to the others that he meets on the course. There should be no collisions or loss of the ball to other players.

d) Mini-Pyramids

Equipment

Six slalom poles, two cones and one ball per player.

Preparation

Two starting cones are set up side by side, five metres apart. Three metres in front of each cone are three slalom poles (1.5 metres apart). The players line up in groups of the same number at the cones.

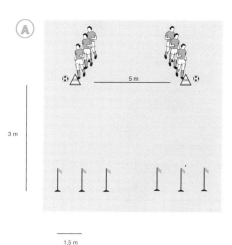

Procedure

Exercises without the ball

Exercise 1:
The players run from the starting cone through the slalom and back to the start again. When the first player is at the middle slalom pole, the next player in his team starts his run.

Exercise 2:
As in Exercise1, except that the players now run once all the way around the central pole in small rapid steps.

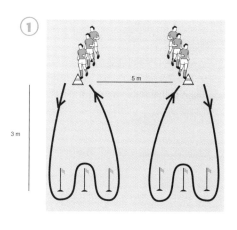

37

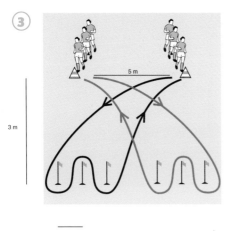

5 m

3 m

1,5 m

Exercise 3:

As in Exercise 1, except that the players now do not run through the slalom pole in front of their own starting cone, but cross over to the other side and run through the slalom there. Finally they cross back over to their own starting cone.

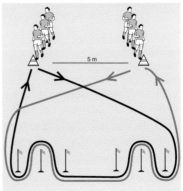

5 m

3 m

1,5 m

Exercise 4:

As in Exercise 3, except that the players now run around all six slalom poles, i.e. including those of the other team, and then back to their own starting cone.

Exercises with the ball

Exercise 5:

The players dribble the ball from the starting cone around the three slalom poles and back to the start again. When the first player is at the middle pole, the next player starts dribbling the ball.

Exercise 6:

As in Exercise 5, except that the players now dribble the ball all the way around the middle pole in the slalom course.

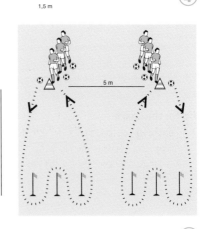

5 m

3 m

1,5 m

Exercise 7:

As in Exercise 5, except that the players now do not dribble the ball through the slalom course in front of their own starting cone, but cross over to that of the other team and dribble the ball through that. Finally they cross back to their own starting cone.

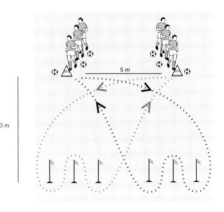

Exercise 8:

As in Exercise 7, except that the players now dribble the ball through all six poles, i.e. including those of the other team, and then return to their own starting cone.

Exercise 9:

A in Exercise 8, except that the players now carry out a feint in the space between the two groups of slalom poles.

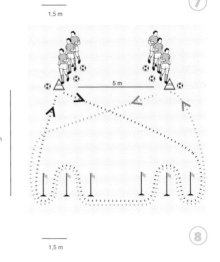

Tip for the coach

• Teaching vision skills: when running or dribbling the ball through the poles, the players should keep their eyes on the ball and on the other players they meet. There should be no collisions or loss of the ball to other players.

2   PASSING

When passing the ball is kicked from one player to another. Passes of various sorts are the basis of modern soccer, which is distinguished by fast and practiced combination playing and a relatively small part of dribbling. Especially in the middle and top grades there is a noticeable tendency towards less contact with the ball by each individual player.

Mainly passes are played by an inside kick. They can also be played with the front, inner or outer instep, as well as different variations (heel, tip, dropkick, hip rotation kick, overhead kick).

A pass with the inside is used mainly for short passes which are not carried out with much force, but very precisely. It is the most frequent form of passes and is used mainly in a controlled build-up, when shifting the game or in wall passes.

Passes using the full instep are used to cover greater distances on the field as this technique allows higher ball speed. Those passes often are used when starting a counter-attack, when shifting the game or by a goalkeeper at a kick-out. Controlled this type of pass can also be used over shorter or medium distances.

For medium distances the ball is very often passed with the inner or outer instep. Since by this technique the ball can be played a bit lateral below the centre of the ball these passes can be carried out with a spin. With this technique a player can play around an opponent, which is useful in free kicks, corner kicks or shifting the game.

- Inside Kick

   The inside of the foot is the part that hits the ball. The playing foot is fixed by drawing up the tiptore to the shin. The standing foot is a foot's width beside the ball.

- Inner instep kick

  The inside of the instep hits the ball. The playing foot must be fixed and the leg must swing forward in front of the standing leg after hitting the ball.

- Full instep kick

  The full instep hits the ball. By tension after the pass or shot towards the ground the leg swings forwards, the foot is fixed upwards.

- Outer instep kick

  The outer instep hits the ball. The foot is turned inwards and is slightly bent. The leg swings forwards sidewards.

Training Forms for "Passing"

a) Passing Games– Sprinting

Equipment

Six cones and one ball per player.

Preparation

Four metres in front of two starting cones (five metres apart) an area of 5 x 2 metres is marked with four cones. In the middle, six metres behind the area the coach stands as a return position.

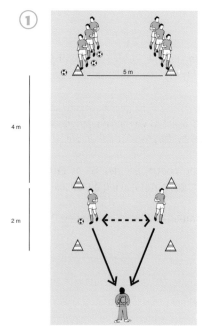

Procedure

Two players with a ball stand opposite each other on the field, passing the ball as directly as possible. The other players, in two teams of the same number, wait at the starting cones.

Exercise 1:

At an acoustic or visual sign from the coach, the two players let the ball roll, sprint towards the coach and clap at him.

Exercise 2:

As in Exercise 1, except that the players now add an extra movement before sprinting towards the coach. This may be a turn, a header imitation, a roll or a run around the cones.

Exercise 3:

A player stands at each of the nearer cones of the marked area and plays direct passes with the first player at the start cone. At a sign from the coach (acoustic/visual) the players on the field let the ball roll, turn around, sprint towards the coach and clap at him.

Exercise 4:

As in Exercise 3, except that the players now add an additional move before sprinting towards the coach. This may be a turn, a header imitation, a roll or a run around the cones.

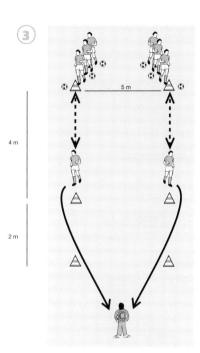

Tips for the coach

- For advanced players the exercises can also be carried out with two balls simultaneously. (Rhythm teaching: playing the balls at the same time or at the same rhythm.)

- Direct passes should only be carried out if this is technically possible after the incoming pass; otherwise the ball should be stopped for a moment.

- During all exercises or game-forms the coach can reduce or increase his distance to the area, so that each player has to run varying distances.

- Exercise or game-forms can also be carried out as competitions: "Who can clap at the coach first?"

b) Wall Passes – Sprinting

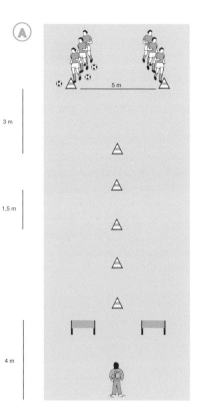

Equipment

Seven cones, two hurdles and one ball for each pair of players.

Preparation

Three metres in front of two starting cones (5 m apart) five cones are set up on centre with a distance of 1,5 m, so that they form four cone goals.

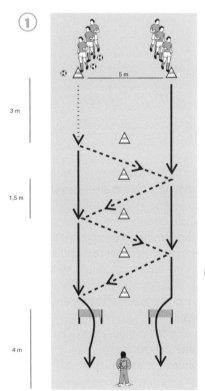

At the far end a hurdle stands on each side behind the last cone. The coach stands four metres behind the hurdles. The players divide into pairs and stand in teams of the same number behind the starting cones.

Procedure

Exercise 1:
The first pair of players in each case passes the ball to each other as directly as possible through the cone goals. After the last pass the players sprint over the hurdles to the coach and clap at him.

Exercise 2:

As in Exercise 1, except that the players now carry out an extra movement after the last pass e.g. a turn, header imitation or a roll. They then sprint over the hurdles to the coach and clap at him.

Exercise 3:

As in Exercise 1, except that the players now play a wall pass at each cone goal.

Exercise 4:

As in Exercise 3, except that the players now carry out an extra movement after the last pass e.g. a turn, a roll or a header imitation.

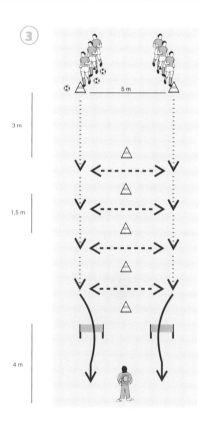

Tips for the coach

- The passing game should be carried out in a technically correct manner without any pressure of time. The players act quickly only after the last pass.
- The players should only pass the ball directly if it is is technically possible after the incoming pass; if not, the ball should be stopped shortly.
- During all exercises and games the coach can increase or reduce the distance between himself and the area with the cones, so that players have various distances to run.
- The cone goals can be increased (making the exercise easier) and reduced in size (making the exercise more difficult).
- Exercise and game-forms can also be carried out without the two hurdles. The players then sprint in a straight line towards the coach.
- Exercise and game-forms can also be carried out as a competition: "Who can clap at the coach first?"

c) Passing Games – Running Round

Equipment

Four cones, four poles and one ball per group.

Preparation

Two cone goals (width: 2,5 m) of two cones each are set up in a distance of 10 m apart. On one side of the playing area four poles are putting across in a row (pole distance 0,5 m). The players stand in two equally-sized teams, one behind the other at the cone goal. The first player in one team has the ball.

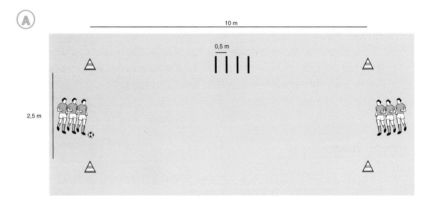

Procedure

Exercise 1:
The players pass the ball to each other directly if possible. After each pass they change sides by running around the right outside to the opposite end. When running over the poles they touch the space in between each pole with at least one foot. On the other side the players change sides while running in a flat sprint.

Exercise 2:
As in Exercise 1, except that the runs are varied when the players change sides. They now run around the poles in slalom or run around them once and then run over them. The players running the flat line add extra movements such as turns, header imitation jumping or a roll etc.

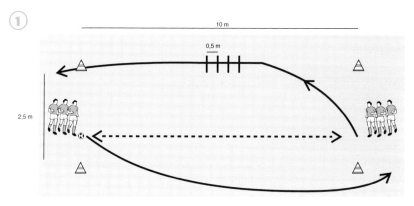

Exercise 3:

As in Exercise 3, but with a variation to the passing game:

- the players throw the balls
- each player in the group on one side has a ball. After passing the ball the players run over the poles and have to perform a given task. The players in the other team take the ball and dribble it to the other side.

Tip for the coach

- The players should only pass the ball directly if it is possible after the incoming pass. Otherwise the ball should be stopped shortly.

d) Pass – Timing

Equipment

Six slalom poles, seven cones and one ball per player.

Preparation

Three metres in front of a start cone a staggered slalom course of six poles is set up (straight and lateral distance 1,5 m each). Laterally staggered behind the slalom course four cones mark an area of three metres sidelines. Ten metres behind the cone area a cone goal (width 3 m) is set up. The players stand at the start cone.

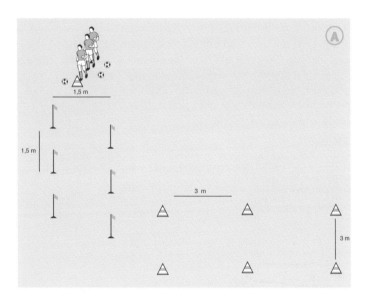

Procedure

Exercise 1:

The players dribble the ball around the slalom course. Then they dribble it through the cone area by dribbling it around two cones in a figure-eight-shaped course. Then they kick the ball into the cone goal following their pass by sprinting through the goal.

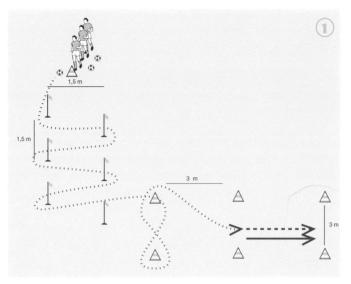

Exercise 2:

The players pass the ball through the centre of the slalom area and run around the slalom course without it. Then they pass the ball again by kicking it through the cone area and through the goal.

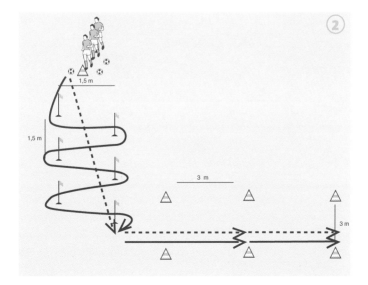

Then the players sprint after the ball (to make things more difficult the goal can be set up laterally to the cone area, so that the players have to pass the ball into the goal directly form a rotation.)

Exercise 3:

As in Exercise 2, except that the players now add an extra movement before passing (such as a turn, a roll or a jump).

Exercise 4:

As in Exercise 2, except that another player now stands behind the slalom and behind the cone area. Instead of passing the ball to themselves the players pass it to the next player. The passing player follows his pass.

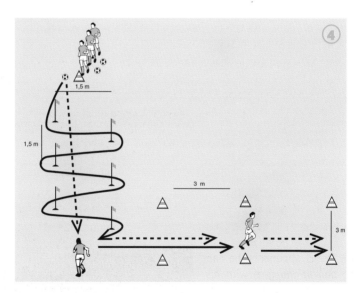

Tip for the coach

- If the first player has dribbled the ball around the slalom, the next players can start dribbling. This reduces the waiting period for each player.

3   GOAL SHOT

The techniques used for goal shots are almost identical to those used in passing (c.f. the chapter on "Passing"). A goal shot can also be called a pass with the intention of scoring a goal. All types of kicks used in passing are also various techniques used to shoot a goal. A goal shot can be carried out with the inside of the foot, the full instep, the inner or outer instep and various other forms such as with the heel, the tiptoe, a dropkick, a hip rotation kick or an overhead kick.

A goal shot with the inside of the foot is mainly used from a short distance, since it can be executed very precisely. However because of the unnatural position of the foot, there are limits to the force that can be used to kick the ball.

Goal shots from greater distances are carried out mostly with the full instep, as this technique allows higher ball speeds. Goal shots with the full instep are used at long distances, for free kicks and for penalty kicks.

Goal shots made from the middle distance are very often made with the inner instep. Since by this technique the ball can be played a bit lateral below the centre of the ball it gets a spin and thus can be played around an opponent. This is often used in free kicks around an opponent wall.

If a player is not sufficiently well-positioned to shoot the ball, e.g. head-on to the goal or with the goal and opposing players in his field of vision, he still has a wide range of goal shot variations kicks to choose from. If the player is standing with his back to his opponents, he can kick the ball at the goal with his heel or by an overhead kick. If he is standing side-on to his opponents' goal and the ball is flying through the air anywhere between knee and hip level, a hip rotation kick is a useful technique.

Various types of shots

- **The Drop-Kick**

  The player hits the ball immediately after it bounces back off the ground with the full or outer instep (a hard shot) or softly with the inside (a soft pass). This foot must be fixed either by tension (instep) or by flexion (inside).

- **The Spin Kick**

  The ball is hit off-centre with the inner or outer instep. By this off-centre contact the ball gets the desired spin.

- **The "Hip-Rotation" Kick**

  Out of a rotation the ball is hit at hip height on the volley with the full instep. The playing foot is tensed and thus fixed. After hitting the ball the playing leg swings far forward.

- **The Overhead Kick**

  The player stands with his back to the goal and while falling backwards hits the ball with the full instep. The take off is with the playing leg. The player then carries out a scissors movement with both legs in order to enable the shot. This can also be carried out more easily by taking off with the standing leg, which makes the scissors movement unnecessary.

Exercises for Goal Shots

a) Running over Poles and Goal Shot

Equipment

Eight poles, three cones, one ball per player and a goal.

Preparation

Fifteen metres in front of a goal two sets of four poles each (pole distance of 0,5 m) are set out in a distances of 3 m. Laterally in the centre of the space in between a cone is set out. To each side of the poles another cone is set out as start and finish marker. The players are standing at the start cone.

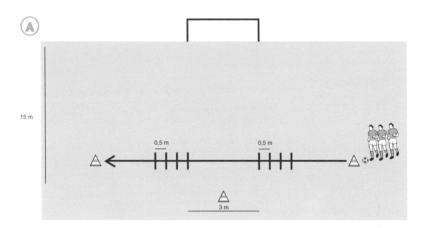

Procedure

Exercises without the ball
The players are running over the poles consecutively, the next player starting when the one in front is in the space between the two sets of poles.

Exercise 1:
The players run over the poles, touching the space between with one foot each.

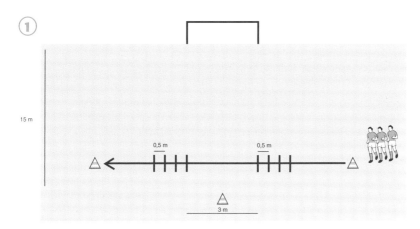

Exercise 2:

As in Exercise1, except that the players now carry out an extra movement in the space between the two sets of poles e.g. a turn, a roll or a header imitation. Then they jump over the next four poles.

Exercise 3:

As in Exercise 1, except that the players now run around the cone in the space between the sets of poles. Then they continue running over the next four poles.

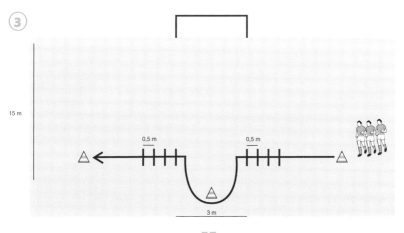

Exercises with the ball

Exercise 4:

The players put out the ball in the space between the two sets of poles. Then they run over the first four poles, touching the space in between with one foot each. In the space between the sets they shoot the ball at the goal. They go on to run over the next four poles, touching the space between with one foot each as well. Then they repeat the exercise from the other side, thus having to shoot goals with each foot alternately.

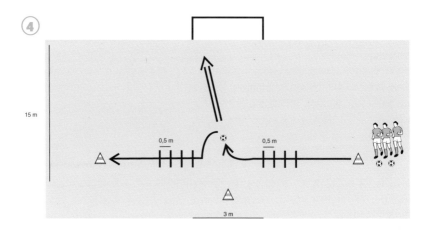

Exercise 5:

As in Exercise 4, except that the players now hold the ball in their hands and shoot it like a goalkeeper's kickout at the goal while in the space between the two sets of poles.

Tip for the coach

Get the players to orient themselves towards the goal before shooting at it by getting their eyes away from the poles and the ball.

b) Dribbling around Cones and Goal Shot

Equipment

Four cones, a goal and one ball per player.

Preparation

15 m in front of a goal an area (sideline 8 m) is marked by four cones. The players are standing in two equally-sized groups at the two far cones of the cone area.

Procedure

Players from each team alternately dribble the ball towards the front cone and shoot at goal. After the shot the players add at the other cone.

Exercise 1:
The players dribble the ball in a straight line from the starting cone towards the front one and shoot at the goal.

Exercise 2:
Before the shot at goal the players pass the ball a few metres in front of them, perform an extra movement, e.g., a turn, a roll or header imitation, and only then shoot at goal.

Exercise 3:
The players pass the ball a few metres in front of them in the direction of the front cone, run after it and, just before they reach it, perform a sideways roll. While still on the ground, they attempt to shoot the ball at the goal.

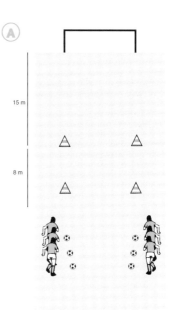

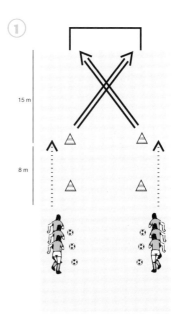

59

Exercise 4:

The players throw the ball towards the first cone (overhead throw), run after the ball and when it has bounced once, shoot it on the volley at the goal.

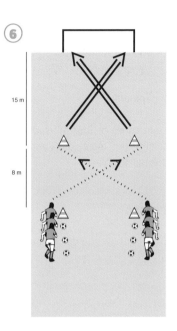

Exercise 5:

As in Exercise 4, except that the players now perform an extra movement (a turn, a roll or a header imitation) and then shoot the ball at the goal after the first ground contact.

Exercise 6:

The ball is now dribbled diagonally towards the first cone. The first two players start dribbling at the same time so that they cross in the middle, and then shoot at the goal out of the rotation.

Tips for the Coach

- In all exercises and game-forms a goalkeeper can be brought into play. All uses as goalkeeper train the individual player in coordination (e.g. two simultaneous goal shots teach the goalie's reaction).
- The players should learn to play and shoot two-footed.
- Give instructions on how shots should be carried out e.g. long or short corner shot, or with a low or high shot.
- Exercise and game-forms can be performed as competitions: "Who can score a goal first, when the first players both start at the same time?"

c) Running around Various Coloured Cones and Goal Shots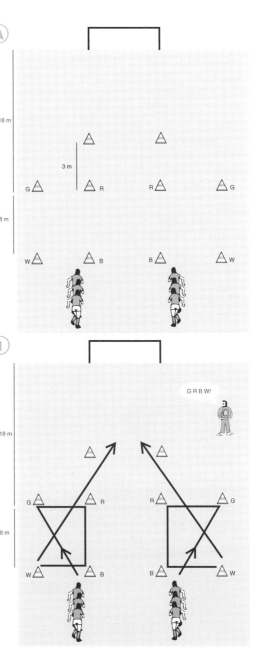

Equipment

Eight cones of four different colours, two more cones and one ball per player.

Preparation

Eight cones stand side-on to, and 18 metres away from a goal. The cones form two areas and have sidelines of eight metres. In both areas each cone has a different colour. Two more cones form a finish line three metres away from the two areas in the direction of the goal. The players stand in two equal-sized teams behind each area.

Procedure

Exercises without the ball

Exercise 1:

The coach calls out a colour combination (e.g. green-red-blue-white). The players start running into each area and with one hand the touch the coloured cones in the order called out by the coach. Then they sprint over the finish line.

Exercise 2:

Besides calling out the colours, the coach also calls out "Change!". At the call "Change!", the players run through the practice area to the other side, touch the coloured cones with one hand in the order called out by the coach and then sprint over the finish line.

Exercise 3:

As in Exercises 1 and 2, except that now the players perform an extra movement (turn, roll or header imitation) before the coach calls out the combination of colours.

Exercises with the ball

Exercise 4:

The players put a ball in front of the practice area. After the coach has called out the colour combination the players run to the cone area, touch the coloured cones in the order called out for and shoot the ball at the goal.

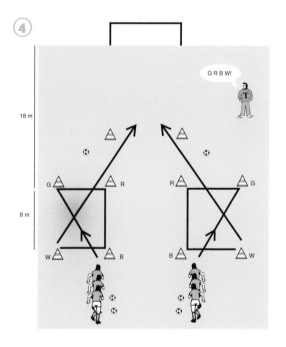

Exercise 5:

As in Exercise 4, except that the players now hold the ball in their hands. After the coach has called out the colours, the players run to the cone area, touch the cones in the order of the colours called out for and shoot the ball at the goal out of their hands.

Tips for the coach

- A goalkeeper can be used in all exercises and game-forms. By this each player is trained in coordination (e.g. two simultaneous goal shots teach the goalie's reaction).
- Depending on the level of the players' performance fewer (easier) or more (more difficult) colours can be called out.
- Exercise and game-forms can be carried out as competitions: "Who can cross the finish line first? Who can score a goal first?"

4   Ball Control

The fact that accurate and fast passing is becoming more and more the dominating technique in soccer leads to the logical conclusion that ball control is gaining a corresponding importance at the same time. It is a feature of every incoming pass, if it is not passed on directly. Soccer-specific technique of ball control is made of stopping and controlling the ball.

Ball control is a basic soccer technique and is used by players in all positions. The goalkeeper takes bad passes from the opposing team or back passes from his own team; defence players intercept passes from their opponents or get involved in the build-up of the game by various combinations of passes. Midfield and offensive players take passes under greater pressure from their opponents in order to build-up an attack. In order to take the ball, the players have a wide range of techniques at their disposal: low and high passes can be controlled or brought down with the foot (sole, inside/outside instep), the thigh, the chest or the head.

Tips on execution

- Move towards the ball before taking it and stop it softly for controlling.
- For taking along the ball, do not stop it completely but pass it directly into the new direction. Take the ball into the space away from on opponent.
- When stopping the ball or taking it along, a body feint can be added.

Exercises of Ball Control Training

a) Ball Control while Running over Poles

Equipment

Six poles, two cones and one ball per player.

Preparation

Two cones are set up 15 metres opposite each other. In the middle between six poles are putting across in a row (distance between poles 0,5 m). The players stand in two teams of the same size at each cone.

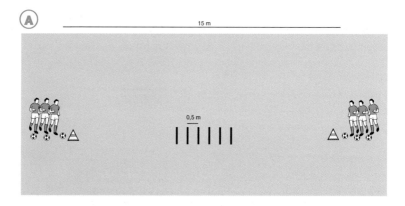

Procedure

Exercise 1:

The first player at each cone runs over the poles without the ball. As soon as he has crossed them he gets a ball passed by the player from the other team. The player brings the ball under control and adds at the other cone. The player who passed runs over the poles to the other cone, and the same action starts again.

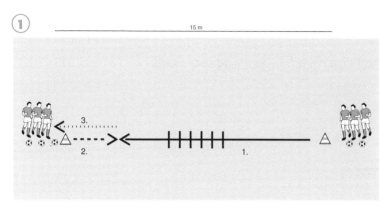

Exercise 2:

As in Exercise 1, except that the first players at each cone start running at the same time, so that each action runs parallel to the other one.

Exercise 3:

Before the first player runs over the poles, he passes the ball to the first player at the opposite cone. This player takes control of the ball and then passes it to the next player at the opposite cone. After every long pass the passers run over the poles.

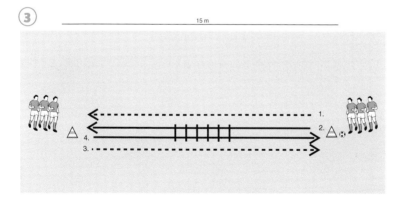

Exercise 4:

As in Exercise 3, except that the first player in each team starts running at the same time, so that each action runs parallel to the other one.

Exercise 5:

The first player at a cone passes the ball to the opposite cone and then starts his run over the poles. After running over the poles, the ball is passed to him, he brings it under control, passes it back and then adds at the cone. The next player starts the action again with a long pass.

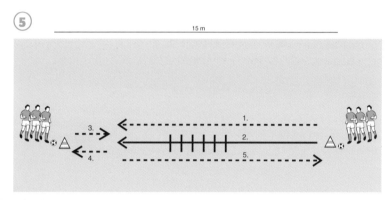

Exercise 6:

As in Exercise 5, except that the action starts at both cones at the same time with two balls (only for advanced players).

Exercise 7:

The first players at each cone start the exercise at the same time. The players dribble the ball around the poles in a clockwise direction and then pass it to the next players at the cones, who bring it under control and also start their dribbling.

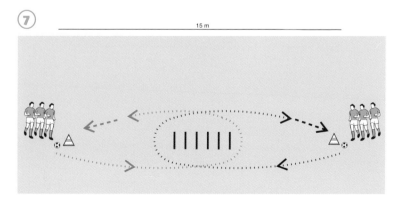

70

Exercise 8:
As in Exercises 1-7, except that instead of passing the ball at ground level, it is either thrown, highly passed out of a player's hand or highly passed from the ground.

Tip for the coach

- These games or exercises can be varied by altering the way the poles are used (running over them backwards, sideways or slalom fashion), varying the distances between the poles or varying the start by including a turn, roll or jump.

b) Ball Control and Dribbling around Poles

Equipment

Five cones, four poles and one ball.

Preparation

Two metres from a starting cone, four more cones (1.5 metres apart) mark a slalom course. Three metres further away four poles are putting across in a row (0.5 metres apart). The coach stands side-on to the field between the cones and the poles. The players stand at the starting cone, the first player has a ball.

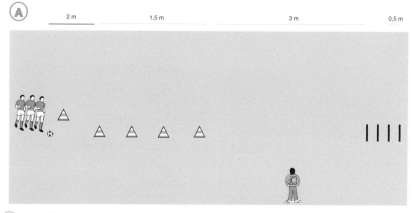

Preparation

Exercise 1:
The first player dribbles the ball around the slalom course. Then he passes the ball to the coach and sprints over the poles, touching the ground between each pole with one foot. After running the slalom course the coach throws the ball to the player who brings it under control and passes it to the next player at the starting cone. This player also brings the ball under control and the action starts again.

Exercise 2:
As in Exercise 1, except that the coach now varies the pass (low, hip-high, high).

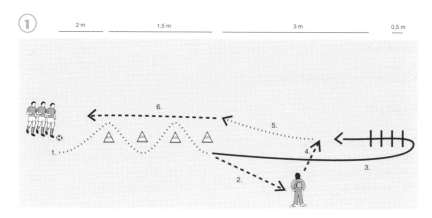

Exercise 3:

As in Exercise 1, except that the player now has to carry out an extra movement, e.g. a turn, a roll or a header, before running around the poles and/or before bringing the ball under his control.

Exercise 4:

As in Exercise 1, except that the ball is passed highly from the starting cone by a goalkeeper's kickout, so that it must be brought down from the air before the dribbling.

Tip for the coach

- Instead of the coach another player can throw or pass the ball. However, this must be done correctly (an overhead throw).

 TECHNIQUE

c) Ball Control in a Goal Area

Equipment

Fourteen cones, four red and four yellow tyres and four balls.

Preparation

Four cones form a 15 square metre practice field. Two cones each, two metres apart and positioned at all four sides of the field, form a goal. Three goals are numbered one to three. Two cones, ten metres behind the non-numbered goal, form a starting goal. Between the starting goal and the non-numbered goal there are put eight different-coloured tyres in two rows. The coach stands outside the practice area. Three players with a ball stand in each of the three numbered goals. The other players add at the starting goal (before the tyres).

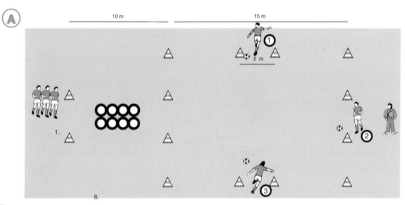

Procedure

Exercise 1:

The first player starts running over the tyres, touching the ground with one foot in each tyre. After the player has run through the non-numbered goal, the coach calls out a number from one to three. The player runs towards the relevant goal, and gets the ball thrown highly by the player standing there. After the player has brought the ball under control, he dribbles it into the goal. The player who threw the ball adds at the starting goal. After the coach's calling out another number, the action starts again.

Exercise 2:

As in Exercise 2, except that the coach now no longer calls out a number but uses his fingers to indicate the number of the relevant goal.

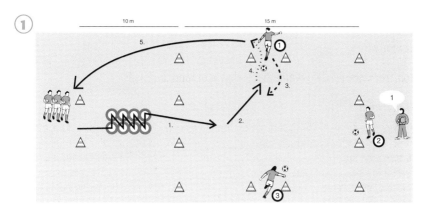

Exercise 3:

As in Exercise 1, except that the coach now calls out two or three numbers or a combination of (e.g.1-3-2-1). The player passes the ball back with a low pass after controlling it at the first cone goals. At the last called cone goal he dribbles into the goal again and replaces the thrower.

Exercise 4:

As in Exercise 1, except that the players now have to run through the tyres in a yellow-red-yellow-red etc. or red-yellow-red-yellow rhythm.

Exercise 5:

As in Exercise 1, except that now the first player at the starting cone also has a ball. He dribbles the ball around the tyres, passes it to the next player and runs over the tyres and brings the ball under control at the numbered cone goals.

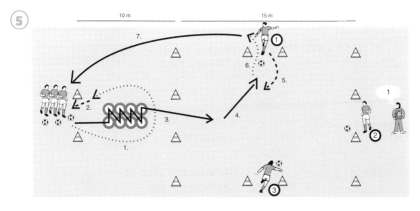

5 Playing Headers

Hitting the ball with one's head is a soccer-related movement used to play high passes. It can be used for passing, scoring a goal, or defence.

Certainly with a quick and accurate combination game in mind usually low passes are used but the fact that attempts to attack are more and more often confronted by a stronger defence means that the use of high crosses is a good idea. Accordingly this requires to learn headers as an attack and a defence technique.

Typical situations in which headers are used: passing along balls kicked out by the goalkeeper, corner kicks, free kicks, crosses or a throw in. As goal shot technique headers are used at corner kicks, free kicks from the wings or crosses. Headers as a defence technique can be used in all positions and situations in which the other team plays the ball highly as pass or goal shot. Even the goalkeeper can use headers as pass or goal shot as a defence technique when defending high bouncing balls outside the penalty area.

Some ways of heading the ball

- From a standing position:
  With the legs in a parallel or in a walking position, hitting the ball with the forehead out of a body stress.

- From rotation in a standing position:
  As above, except that when moving his body forward, the player turns his torso in the direction the ball is passed or kicked at.

- From a two-footed takeoff (from a standing position):
  After a two-footed takeoff, like from a standing position, the player heads the ball at the highest point of his jump.

- From a one-footed takeoff (out of running):
  As above, except that the player has to coordinate his running up with the takeoff and the header.

- From jumping with rotation:
  After the takeoff the player turns his body in the direction he heads the ball to.

- From a flying-dive as "flying-header" :
  The player jumps and dives towards the ball (a flying dive).

Exercises for Training Headers

a) Header Competition

Equipment

Two cone goals and one ball for every pair of players.

Preparation

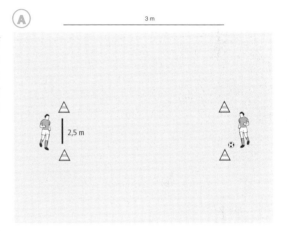

Two cone goals (width of 2.5 metres) are set up three metres opposite each other. A player stands in each goal, one with the ball.

Procedure

Exercise 1:
One player throws the ball up to himself and tries to score a goal into the opposite goal. The player in this goal acts as goalkeeper and tries to block it.

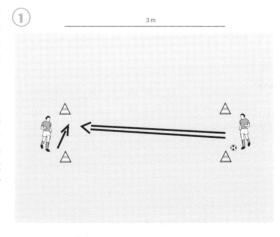

Exercise 2:
As in Exercise1, except that the players no longer throw the ball to themselves but head it at the goal after the partner has thrown it.

Exercise 3:

As in Exercise 1, except that the coach now introduces the concept of a "change" into the training. At the command "Change!" from the coach the players have to change sides immediately and then continue playing.

Tips for the coach

- Don't get the players to carry out too many headers; add in sufficient breaks into the training session.
- For basic training use lighter balls or soft balls for header training.

b) Flying Headers

Equipment

A cone, a mini goal and one ball per player.

Preparation

A starting cone stands 5 metres away from a minigoal. The coach stands behind the minigoal and acts as "thrower-in". Each player stands with a ball at the starting cone.

Procedure

Exercise 1:
The first player throws the ball to the coach, who then throws it back over the minigoal to the player. The latter has to head the ball into the minigoal.

Exercise 2:
As in Exercise 1, except that the player adds an extra movement such as a turn or a roll, before heading the ball.

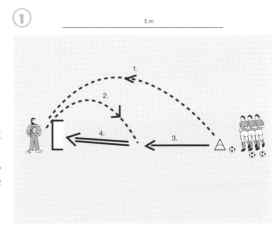

Exercise 3:
A in Exercise 1, except that the player now has to head the ball back to the coach and perform a turn. The coach then throws the ball again and the player heads the ball as a flying header into the minigoal.

Tips for the coach

- Don't get the players to head the ball too often; add sufficient breaks into the training session.
- For basic training use lighter balls or soft balls for header training.

c) Header and Goal Shot

Equipment

Eight poles, six cones, a goal and one ball per player.

Preparation

Five metres in front of each goal post four poles each are putting in a row (distance between the poles 0,5 m). Three metres side-on of each goal post a starting cone is put up. Another cone is five metres in front of each starting cone. 10 m in front of the goal a cone goal (width: 3 m) is put up. The players stand with the ball at the starting cones beside the goal posts. One more player stands at each of the two other cones in front of the starting cones.

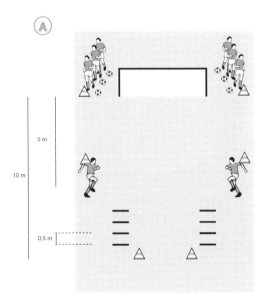

Procedure

Exercise 1:

The players in front of the starting cones get the ball thrown at and head it back accurately. Then they sprint over the poles into the cone goal, touching the ground between each pole with one foot.

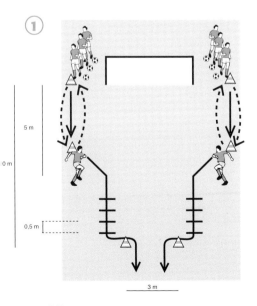

85

Exercice 2:

As in Exercise 1, except that before heading the ball, the players lie in prone position and perform a complete body roll.

Exercice 3:

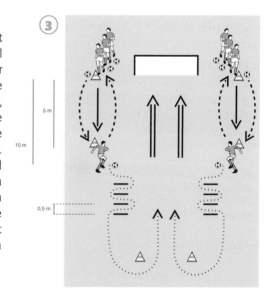

As in Exercise 1, except that the players heading the ball now have an extra ball. After the header they dribble the second ball around the posts, dribble it round one of the cone goals and out of the rotation shoots at the goal. This exercise can be carried out either as a competition with a starting sign (acoustic/visual) from the coach ("Who can shoot at goal first?") or by one team then the other alternately.

Exercice 4:

As in Exercise 3, except that the players now hold the ball in their hands, and after throwing it into the air play it to themselves by a header over the poles. After running over the poles out of a rotation the players shoot the ball at the goal.

Tips for the coach

- Carry out the games and exercises in competition form: "Who can clap at the coach first? Who can score a goal first?"
- At all exercises and games with a final shot at goal a goalkeeper can be used. By playing as goalkeeper each player is trained in coordination (e.g. two simultaneous goal shots teach the goalie's reaction).

6   Playing as Goalkeeper

In soccer the goalkeeper has an outstanding position. The goalkeeper is the only player who is allowed to catch and play the ball with his hands inside his own penalty area. As well he is usually the last defence player who blocks shots at goal from the opposing team, which is his main task overall.

However the goalkeeper should by no means be regarded as just a defence player. On the contrary, of all positions this one is very well suited for determining the rhythm of the game. By various types of passes he can determine the speed of the build-up of an attack after blocking an attack of the opposing team. For example: he can pass the ball accurately to an own defence player, throw it into his own midfield or kick it out into the opponents' half of the field.

The range of defence actions contains picking up and catching the ball, rolling away, diving, jumping, turning the ball away, punching, and blocking with the feet. The ball can come up to the goalkeeper low, hip-high, high, frontally or from the side.

For playing as a goalkeeper, the following basic techniques are important

- The basic position

  The goalkeeper stands parallel with his feet hip-width apart, the body-weight on the balls of his feet. The knees and hips are bent and the torso is slightly bent forward. The arms hang down vertically but the elbows are bent at an angle of 90° with the insides of the hands facing each other. The player keeps his eyes to the field.

- Jumping and diving

  There are two different types of jump used by the goalkeeper. He either takes off two-footed, i.e. from a standing position, or off one leg, i.e. after running up one or a few steps. When jumping out of a forward movement the heel is landing first, at a backward movement first the forefoot then the heel, at a sideway movement first the inside (at a straddle stride) or the outside (at a cross stride) of the foot, then the heel and the toes. When diving, the goalkeeper must land smoothly; he can do this by the right curved body position when rolling backwards, sideways and forward.

- Catching the ball

  Regarding the catching of the ball a distinction is made between catching "low incoming balls", "incoming balls at hip-height" and "high incoming balls".

In all techniques it is important to approach the ball with the hands or the arms and to draw the ball quickly to one's chest after catching it.

• Taking up the ball

A distinction is made between "Taking up frontally incoming balls", "Lateral taking up

of side incoming balls", "Taking up and bouncing away", "Taking up low and hip-high balls when diving sideways up or down". In all taking up techniques the

goalkeeper must bring his body behind the ball and at the moment of contact must move his arms in the direction in which the ball is going to.

• Turning the ball away

The goalkeeper must try to get the hand closest to the ball behind it as quickly as possible.

- Punching the ball

  The goalkeeper can punch away the ball with one or both hands by stretching out his arms and jerking his torso sharply.

- Diving or falling

  Rolling sideways, falling backwards, diving or falling forwards, diving sideways and forwards, and backwards are all parts of diving and falling techniques. When using all these techniques the goalkeeper must approach the ball and secure it on his chest.

- Throwing before the feet

  The goalkeeper must keep his eyes on the ball and must throw himself on it.

- Holding balls when being attacked

  The goalkeeper must have his arms above his opponent, thus getting it first. He must also use his body according to the rules when being attacked by his opponents e.g. raising up his knee which is near to his opponent.

- Playing skills

  The goalkeeper must also be trained in the skills of ball control, passing, heading and tackling (c. f. Training for Field Players).

- Build-up of an attack

  When building up an attack the goalkeeper must master throwing techniques (rolling, swinging throws sideways and overhead), the kickout (on the volley and as dropkick) and the goal kick.

Exercises for Training the Goalkeeper

a) The Basic Position

Equipment

Seven cones and one ball per player.

Preparation

A slalom course consisting of four cones, each 1.5 metres apart, is set up two metres away from a starting cone. One metre away from the end of the slalom course is a goal marked by two more cones (width: 4 m). The goalkeepers stand with a ball at the starting cone, the coach stands behind the cone goal.

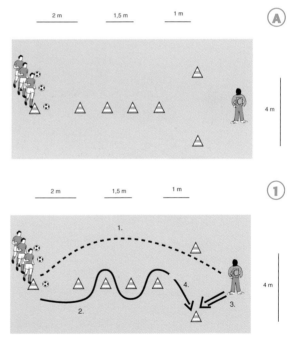

Procedure

Exercise 1:
The first goalkeeper kicks the ball to the coach. Then he runs around the slalom. At the end of the slalom he takes up the goalkeeper's basic position in the goal as quickly as possible and tries to hold the ball which the coach kicks at him.

Exercise 2:
As in Exercise 1, except that the goalkeeper now performs an extra movement in front of the second and fourth cone in the slalom course, e.g. a turn, a roll or a jump.

Exercise 3:

As in Exercise 1, except that the goalkeeper now performs a goalkeeper's roll after the slalom, gets up quickly again and takes up the basic position.

Exercise 4:

The goalkeeper dribbles the ball around the slalom (this teaches field techniques). Then he kicks it to the coach, performs a goalkeeper's roll, tries to take up the basic position in the cone goal as quickly as possible and to hold the ball which the coachs kicks at him.

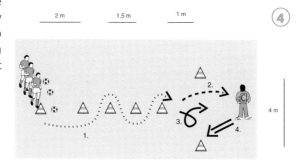

b) Diving for Low Balls/Diving by Numbers

Equipment

Four Soccer Balls.

Preparation

The four soccer balls are put down in a 4 m x 4 m square. Each ball is given a number from 1 to 4. The coach stands outside the practice area. The goalkeeper stands in basic position in the centre between the four balls.

Procedure

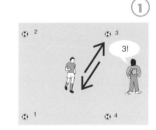

Exercise 1:

The coach calls out a number. The goalkeeper dives onto the corresponding ball and secures it underneath his body. Then he returns to his original position and dives onto the next ball given by the coach.

Exercise 2:

As in Exercise 1, except that the coach now calls out a combination of numbers indicating the balls the goalkeeper has to dive onto. For example, "4-3-1-3" means that the goalkeeper has to dive onto balls number 4,3,1,and 3 one after the other.

Exercise 3:

As in Exercise 2, except that the goalkeeper now carries out an extra movement (a turn, a roll or a jump) before diving onto the balls.

Tip for the coach

• Change the numbering of the cones regularly so that the goalkeeper has to reorientate himself and adjust to a new situation.

c) Catching Hip-high and High Balls/Running a Slalom

Equipment

Two cones, five poles and a ball.

Preparation

Five poles are put out parallel in a row, each one metre apart. On each side of the poles, three metres away, is a starting cone. The coach stands with the ball five metres side-on to the posts. The goalkeepers stand at the starting cones.

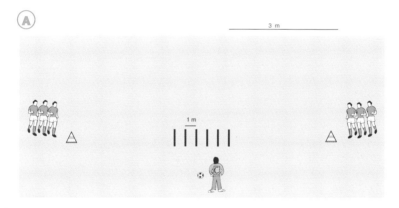

Procedure

Exercise 1:
The first goalkeepers at each cone do a side-gallop over the poles, touching the ground between each pole with one foot. The goalkeeper that started from the right-handed cone runs over the posts behind the other one in front. Both goalkeepers keep their eyes on the coach.

Exercise 2:
As in Exercise 1, except that when both goalkeepers are in the middle of the poles, the coach throws the ball at hip-height to the goalkeeper in front, who should catch it and throw it back to the coach. If he can not catch the ball, the rear goalkeeper must be ready to catch it himself.

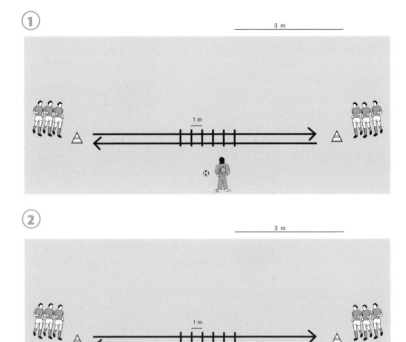

Exercise 3:

As in Exercise 2, except that the coach now throws the ball highly to the goalkeepers.

Exercise 4:

As in Exercise 2, except that the goalkeepers now run in a side-on gallop over the posts with their backs to the coach. The coach then gives a command, at which the goalkeepers direct their gaze at him, who then throws the ball at hip-height to them.

Exercise 5:

As in Exercise 2, except that the coach throws the ball high to the players.

Exercise 6:

As in Exercise 2, except that the running course is varied. The goalkeepers run over the first two poles at a side-on gallop, run back in the same manner, and then run - also at a side-on gallop – to the other side. The coach throws over the ball twice at hip-height. The front goalkeeper has to hold the first ball when he has run over the first two poles; the coach throws the second ball when both goalkeepers run over the centre of the poles.

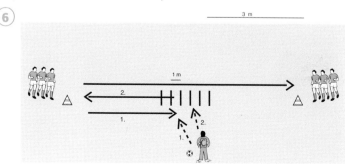

Exercise 7:
As in Exercise 6, except that the coach now throws the ball highly to the goalkeepers.

Exercise 8:
As in Exercise 2, except that the course is varied again. The goalkeepers run around the slalom keeping their eyes on the coach. The goalkeeper that ran from the pole on the right, runs into the slalom from the rear, the other goalkeeper does the same from the front, so that they do not collide. The coach throws the ball at hip-height to the goalkeepers when they both are about in the middle of the slalom course.

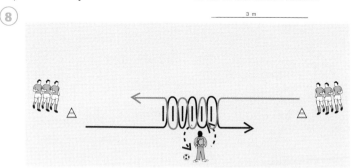

Exercise 9:
As in Exercise 8, except that the coach now throws the ball to both goalkeepers at hip-height several times.

Exercise 10: As in Exercises 8 and 9, except that the coach now throws the ball highly to the goalkeepers.

B) Main Focus: Tactics

The term "tactics" means all organised measures aimed at achieving the objectives of soccer. The basic idea of a soccer game consists of both objectives: to score goals into the opponents' goal and to prevent the opposing team from scoring a goal. Correspondingly there are tactical measures that can be used when attacking and when defending. These can be subdivided into three areas:

- Tactics used by a single player – individual tactics
- Tactics used by two or more players – group tactics
- Tactics used by the whole team – team tactics

Individual Tactics
Individual tactics consist of all directed and planned actions in attacking and defending actions by a single player in typical playing situations. In contrast to soccer techniques with its precise motion, tactics describes each of the principles to be considered when using techniques.

Group Tactics
Group tactics consist of all attacking and defending actions used by an individual player being supported by other defence or attack players of his team. Skills and abilities in individual tactics are the prerequisites for being able to perform within a group tactic.

Team Tactics
The term of team tactics means the tactical plan of a team, by which individual and group tactical measures own goal scoring opportunities are prepared and the opposing team's opportunities to score a goal are prevented or blocked.

Tactics used in defence and attack have an effect on each other. Thus the theory of attack and defence tactics is explained first, but at the end of this chapter exercises and games can be found which teach both areas together.

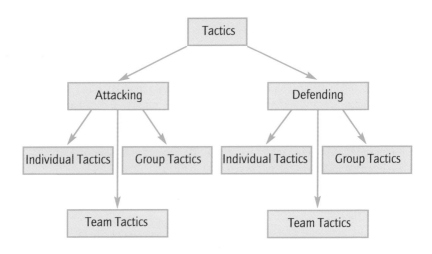

Tactics

Attacking → Individual Tactics, Group Tactics, Team Tactics

Defending → Individual Tactics, Group Tactics, Team Tactics

1   Attacking

Individual attacking tactics are all movements carried out by the individual player with and without the ball. This includes dribbling, passing, goal shots, ball control, headers as well as free running and offering for taking the ball. Also included are the special goalkeeping techniques which are used to prepare the build-up of an attack by one's own team – in other words, those techniques leading to a goal-shot opportunity. The previous chapter dealt especially with the precise description of the movements used when attacking. The following describes in more detail where these can be used and the principles of their use.

> **Individual Tactics**
>
> Dribbling; Passing; Goal Shot; Ball Control; Header;
> Free Running/Offering
> Goalkeeping Techniques
>
> Objective: Preparation for Scoring a Goal

Attacking group tactics means the composition of tactical skills and abilities of individual players. Some players use their individual skills and abilities together in order to score a goal or to perform on the field in accordance with the object of the game. The mastery of tactics on the part of individual players is an absolute prerequisite for the use of group tactics. A combination of all the various forms of individual techniques in dribbling, passing, free running and offering results in the fluent teamwork that leads to the objective of creating opportunities for scoring a goal.

> **Group Tactics**
>
> Space division/Changing Positions/Standard Combinations
> (e.g. Running Behind, Crossing, Wall Passes)
>
> Objective: Scoring Goals

Team attacks are concerned with the composition of individual and group skills and abilities in order to prepare for a goal shot.

Team Tactics			
Frontal Attack	Counterattack	Wing Attack	Shifting the Centre of Play
	Variability	Playing for Time	Standard Situations
		Object: Scoring Goals	

2 Defending

Individual tactics in defence are all movements of the individual player with and without the ball. These include defence tactics used against opposing players dribbling the ball, positional playing in order to prevent the opponent's combination game, the use of defending feints and the use of various tackling techniques.

Individual Tactics	
Defending against dribbles	Preventing the opponent's combination game
Objective: Preventing of goal opportunities	

Defending group tactics means the composition of tactical skills and abilities of individual players. Some players use their individual skills and abilities as a group in order to prevent the other team from scoring goals. The mastery of individual tactics is an absolute prerequisite for being able to perform within a group tactic.

Group Tactics		
Staggering	Shifting	Adjusting
Objective: Preventing of Scoring Goals		

Team tactical defence measures means the composition of tactical skills and abilities of individual players and the group in order to prevent the opposing team from scoring goals.

Team Tactics	
Marking Systems	Pressing/Forechecking
Drawing back	Offside Trap
Standard Situations	
Objective: Preventing of Scoring Goals	

Exercises for the Attack and the Defence

a) One-on-one Crosswise

Equipment

Twelve cones and one ball per pair of players.

Preparation

Four cones are used to form a square playing field 20 metres long. There is a two metre cone goal in the middle of each sideline. The players line up outside the field in teams of equal size beside the goals.

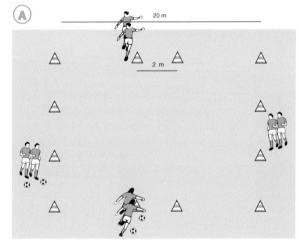

Procedure

Exercise 1:

The first players at each goal go onto the field. Each pair has a ball. At a sign (acoustic/visual) from the coach, the players play one-on-one on their cone goals.

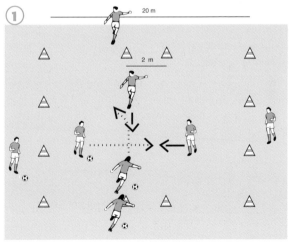

The player with the ball is the attacker. If his opponent gets possession of the ball, he can score a goal at the opposite goal. The game lasts until the ball is either "out" or a goal is scored or the coach ends the game (maximum playing time: 30 seconds). Afterwards the next pairs of players start their 1:1 on the pitch.

Exercise 2:

As in Exercise 1, except that one pair of players passes the ball to each other, while the other one throw the ball to each other. At a command from the coach (acoustical/visual) both pairs of players start the one-on-one game again. Both pairs stand crosswise.

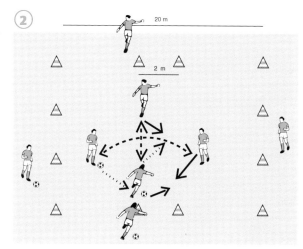

Exercise 3:

As in Exercise 1, except that both pairs of players pass the ball between themselves at the same time, taking care that the balls do not collide when being passed. At a sign from the coach both pairs recommence the one-on-one game, standing crosswise.

Exercise 4:

As in Exercise 1, except that each pair now has two balls. Each member of the pair passes the ball to his team mate, throwing him the other ball at the same time. At a command from the coach both pairs restart the one-on-one (this requires a high level of abilities). The attacker and the defender have been previously determined, so that each pair leaves one ball on the ground at the sign from the coach. Both pairs stand crosswise.

Tips for the coach
- When tackling, each pair should keep an eye on the other pair in order to avoid colliding on the field.
- During the coordination exercises the players must pay attention that the balls do not collide on the field.

b) "Mirror" Running

Equipment

Eight cones, a goal and one ball per player.

Preparation

Eight cones form two square playing fields of 3 m sidelines which are 3 m apart. 15 m behind there is a goal on centre. One player stands in each pitch.

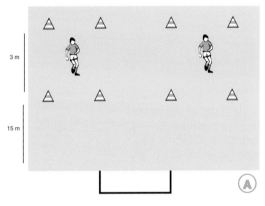

Procedure

Exercise 1:
The player in one pitch gives the lead, running in a straight line, diagonally and to the side between the cones. The player in the other pitch has to copy this pattern (="mirror").

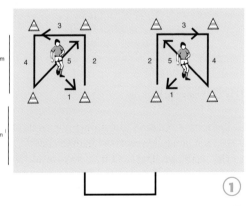

Exercise 2:
As in Exercise 1, except that the leading runner includes additional movements while running e.g. turns, rolls or jumps.

Exercise 3:
As in Exercise 1, except that the coach now gives a starting signal, at which both players sprint towards the coach. The coach stands six metres away at a centre point between the square fields.

Exercise 4:

As in Exercise 1, except that the players now dribble the ball instead of only running.

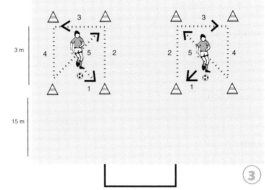

Exercise 5:

As in Exercise 3, except that both players have a ball. At a command from the coach, the players attempt to score a goal instead of clapping at the coach.

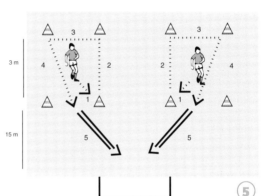

Tips for the coach

- The players must keep their eyes on each other all the time while orientating to each other. This enables them to move forwards, backwards and sideways.
- The leading player must always wait briefly at each cone so that the other player can keep up with him.
- These exercises can also be performed as competitions: "Who can be the first to clap at the coach or to score a goal?"

c) Running in a Circle and One-on-one

Equipment

Eight tyres, eight poles, two cones and one ball per player.

Preparation

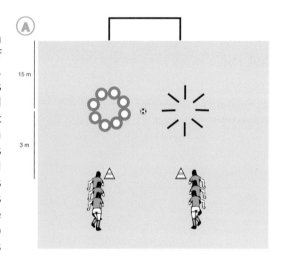

Eight tyres are put in a circle 15 metres in front of one of the goal posts. Beside the tyres, 15 metres in front of the other goal post, eight poles are put down in a circle form. As a starting point two cones stand three metres behind the tyres and the posts respectively. A ball lies between the tyres and the posts. The players line up in two equal-sized teams behind the cones.

Procedure

Exercise 1:
Each of the players runs through the tyre and the pole circle, putting one foot on the ground between each tyre or pole. At a command from the coach (acoustic/visual) the players run towards the ball and try to score a goal out of a one-on-one situation.

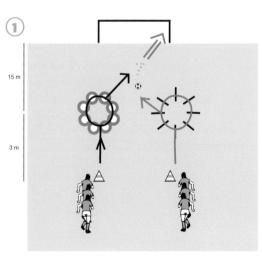

Exercise 2:

As in Exercise 1, except that at a sign from the coach, the players now change the manner in which they run e.g. forwards, backwards or sideways.

Exercise 3:

As in Exercise 1, except that the coach introduces the command "Change!". At this command the players change the running direction.

Exercise 4:

As in Exercise 1, except that the coach now introduces the command "Other side!". On this command the players shift from one course to the other.

Exercise 5:

As in Exercise 1, except that the coach now mixes up all commands: "Forwards!", Backwards!", "Sideways!", "Change!" or "Change sides!".

d) One-on-One Race

Equipment

Nine cones, three hurdles, a goal and one ball per pair of players.

Preparation

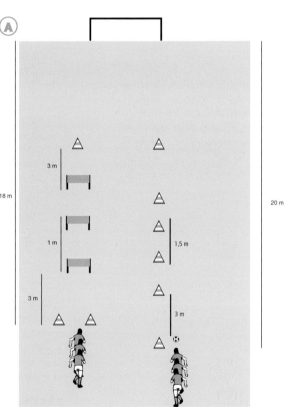

Eighteen metres in front of one of the goal posts a cone goal is put up, twenty metres in front of the other goal post a starting cone is put up. Three metres in front of the cone goal 3 hurdles are put up (1 m distance between). Another cone stands 3 m behind the last hurdle. Three metres in front of the starting cone four other cones (1,5 m distance between) mark a slalom course, another 3 m behind an additional cone is put up. The players stand in equal-sized groups at the starting cone and in the cone goal. Each player at the starting cone has a ball.

Procedure

Exercise 1:

At a sign from the coach both players begin the exercise simultaneously. The player at the cone goal runs around it in a figure-of-eight, runs over the three hurdles and after passing the last cone becomes defender. The player on the other side dribbles the ball in a slalom around the four cones and, after passing the last cone, tries to score a goal out of the one-on-one against the defender.

Exercise 2:

As in Exercise 1, except that the players now throw the ball to each other. The player in possession of the ball at the command of the coach lets it drop onto the ground and takes it through the slalom course. The other player runs as a defender through the other course.

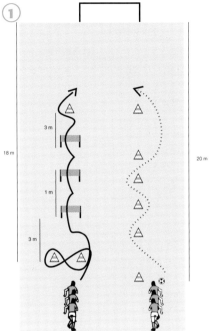

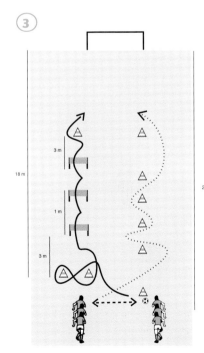

Exercise 3:

As in Exercise 2, except that the players pass the ball to each other.

Exercise 4:

As in Exercise 2, except that the players now head the ball to each other. This demands a high performance level.

🛈 Tip for the coach

• When gaining possession of the ball the defending player can also score a goal. The game lasts until either a goal is scored, the ball is "out" or it is laid down that every player has only one chance at attack (this increases the pressure on each player to be precise at the first time).

Key to Symbols

player, goalkeeper

coach

ball

pole

cones

slalom poles

tyre

hurdle

running path

direction of pass

dribble path

high pass, throw

goal shot, header

LITERATURE

ASMUS, S.: Koordinative Fähigkeiten - Die Basis für den Fußball.
Teil 1 In: Fußballtraining 15 (1997) 7/8, 48 – 56.
Teil 2 In: 15 (1997) 9, 38-45.

ASMUS, S./HÖNL, M./PIEKARSKI, V.: Fußballtraining für Kinder und Jugendliche.
Niedernhausen 1994.

BAUER, G.: Ball- und Körperbeherrschung in allen Spielsituationen.
In: Fußballtraining 15 (1997) 9, 34-37.

BIERMANN, S./THEUNE MEYER, T.: So macht Athletiktraining Spaß!
Gymnastikprogramme der Frauennationalmannschaft zur Verbesserung von
Kraft und Koordination.
In: Fußballtraining 15 (1997) 11/12, 41-48.

BUSCHMANN, J./KOLLATH, E./TRITSCHOKS, H.-J.: Gezielt trainieren – erfolgreich
spielen. Kissing 2000.

DARGATZ, T.: Fußball-Konditionstraining – Koordination und Rehabilitation.
München 1997.

DITGENS, F.: Das Ziel: elegante Bewegungen und variable Techniken. Das
Konditionstraining der B- und A-Junioren von Bayer 04 Leverkusen.
In: Fußballtraining 17 (1999) 3, 17-22.

FRANK, G.: Koordinative Fähigkeiten im Schwimmen. Schorndorf 1996.

GABRIEL, S.: Das Training der koordinativen Fähigkeiten im F- bis D-Jugendalter.
In: Fußballtraining 9 (1991) 1, 11-16; (1991) 2, 27.

GROSSER, M./NEUMAIER, A.: Techniktraining. München/Wien/Zürich 1982.

HASLER, H.-R.: Zielgerichtete Vervollkommnung der koordinativen Fähigkeiten im Vereinssport der 7- bis 13jährigen. In: Magglingen 46 (1989) 9, 7-11.

HASLER, H.-R.: Zielgerichtete Vervollkommnung der koordinativen Fähigkeiten im Vereinsfußball. Aus: NAUL, R./SCHMIDT, W. (Red.): Beiträge und Analysen zum Fußballsport 2: Referate zu den Tagungen der dvs-Kommmission Fußball 1987 und 1988 in Duisburg. Clausthal-Zellerfeld 1989, 83-100.

HEINZEL, A./KOCH, P./STRAKERJAHN, V.: Koordinationstraining im Tennis. Sindelfingen 1997.

KRAUSPE, D./MALORNY, S./RIECK, J.: Theoretische und methodische Positionen zur Ausbildung koordinativer Fähigkeiten im Fußballsport.
In: Wissenschaftliche Zeitschrift der DHfK, Leipzig 27 (1986) 2, 32-51.

KOLLATH, E.: Techniktraining. Aachen 1991.

LIESEN, H.: Physiologische Entscheidungshilfen für das Techniktraining – Thesen. Aus: BUNDESINSTITUT FÜR SPORTWISSENSCHAFT (Hg.): Theorie und Praxis des Techniktrainings. Köln 1988, S. 169-171.

MEINEL, K./SCHNABEL, G.: Bewegungslehre – Sportmotorik. Berlin (Ost) 1987.

MENZE, B.: Praxis: Koordinationsschulung im Nachwuchsbereich. Jugendspieler des FC Schalke 04. In: BDFL Journal 2 (1997) 14, 30-35.

PABST, K.: Koordination – das neue Training – Interessante Übungsformen für ein Koordinationstraining innerhalb verschiedener Altersklassen.
In: Fußballtraining 14 (1996) 9, 62-68.

PABST, K./GREIBER, P.: Koordination – das neue Training – Interessante Übungsformen für ein Koordinationstraining innerhalb verschiedener Altersklassen. In: Fußballtraining 14 (1996) 10, 49-51.

PABST, K.: Koordination – das neue Training – Interessante Übungsformen für ein Koordinationstraining innerhalb verschiedener Altersklassen.
In: Fußballtraining 15 (1997) 7+8, 57-63.

PABST, K./SIMON, F.: Koordination – das neue Torhütertraining. Altersgemäße
Übungs- und Spielformen für das Torhütertraining.
In: Fußballtraining 16 (1998) 7, 30-35.

PETER, R.: Mit besserem Laufen zum attraktiveren Spiel.
Teil 1: Trainingsformen für eine interessante Schulung der Laufkoordination.
In: Fußballtraining 15 (1997) 7/8, 65-68. Teil 2: H. 9, 25-32.

WEINECK, J.: Das Training der koordinativen Fähigkeit im Fußball.
In: BDFL Journal 9 (1998) 16, 18-21 und 4 (1999) 17, 3-6.

WEINECK, J.: Optimales Fußballtraining. Balingen 1998.

WYZNIKIEWICZ-KOPP, Z.: Ausprägung koordinativer Fähigkeiten bei
unterschiedlicher sportlicher Ausbildung.
In: Theorie und Praxis der Körperkultur 38 (1989) Beiheft 2. 59-61.

PHOTO AND ILUSTRATION CREDITS

Cover photo: Philippka-Sportverlag, Münster
Photos: Krisztina Erkenrath
Illustrations: Lars Banka
Cover design: Birgit Engelen

Soccer with Kids

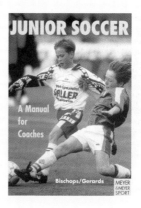

Klaus Bischops/
Heinz-Willi Gerards
**Coaching Tips for
Children's Soccer**

Klaus Bischops/
Heinz-Willi Gerards
Junior Soccer
A Manual for Coaches

Coaching Tips for Children's Soccer is a complete guide for ensuring that young players get the most out of the game – psychologically, socially and physically. Starting with the belief that fun and self discovery are the most important aspects of any sporting activity for children up to the age of 10, the book covers the basic principles of child development and details 60 play-oriented training units which can be utilised by teachers, parents and others working with this age group.

In this book soccer coaches and teachers will find around 100 complete training units for youth-work in clubs. Each unit contains a warm-up section, a section on the main emphasis in the training unit and a specific "winding-down" section with a game. The book begins with the training units for 5-10 year-old children and ends with suggestions for the teenagers (age 16-18).

128 pages
10 photos, 3 figures
Paperback, 11.5 x 18 cm
ISBN 3-89124-529-7
£ 5.95 UK/$ 8.95 US/
$ 12.95 CDN

168 pages
29 photos, 70 figures
Paperback, 14.8 x 21 cm
ISBN 1-84126-000-2
£ 12.95 UK/$ 17.95 US/
$ 25.95 CDN

MEYER
& MEYER
SPORT

MEYER & MEYER Verlag | Von-Coels-Straße 390 | D-52080 Aachen, Germany | Fax + + 49 (0)2 41 - 9 58 10-10

Soccer Know-how

Klaus Bischops/
Heinz-Willi Gerards
**Soccer – Warming-up
and Warming-down**

In this book the authors provide
some 35 programmes for proper warming-up and warming-
down for soccer. The pro-
grammes are full of variety
to avoid monotony and are
based around the game of
soccer itself, within a team
situation. The book proceeds
from a basic understanding of
the needs of every individual to
stretch and ease their muscles
and tendons, through a series
of simple games and exercises
using the football and other
aids.

136 pages
22 photos, 172 figures
Paperback, 14.8 x 21 cm
ISBN 1-84126-014-2
**£ 8.95 UK/$ 14.95 US/
$ 20.95 CDN**

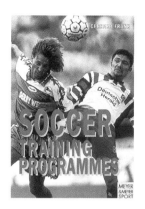

Gerhard Frank
**Soccer
Training Programmes**

Soccer Training Programmes
contains a collection of 96 de-
tailed plans designed to be
used by amateur coaches.
Each programme is based on
knowledge and techniques
developed in professional
soccer and other sports which
have been adapted to the
specific conditions and needs
of the amateur game. In clear
and concise chapters "Soccer
Training Programmes" also
provides an overview of the key
aspects of a coach's work,
including physical training, skill
development, tactics and
psychological preparation.

216 pages
Numerous photos and figures
Paperback, 14.8 x 21 cm
ISBN 3-89124-556-4
**£ 12.95 UK/$ 17.95 US/
$ 25.95 CDN**

MEYER & MEYER Verlag | Von-Coels-Straße 390 | D-52080 Aachen, Germany | Fax: ++49(0)241-9 58 10-10

Out now!

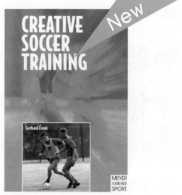

Klaus Bischops/
Heinz-Willi Gerards
**Soccer –
One-on-One**

Systematic and deliberate training in proper one-on-one be-
haviour is an indispensable
element of modern soccer
training. This book is designed
to do justice to the great sig-
nificance of the one-one-one
situation in soccer. With
competence and in great
detail the authors describe
everything you need to know
about that specific situation.

160 pages
Two-colour print
21 photos, 88 figures
Paperback, 14.8 x 21 cm
ISBN 1-84126-013-4
£ 12.95 UK/$ 17.95 US/
$ 25.95 CDN

Gerhard Frank
**Creative Soccer
Training**

In 40 different points of emphasis
in training the book describes
technique, tactical and fitness
training according to the game
method. The aim of the book is
playful structuring of training in
order to return the focus of
soccer to game creativity,
imagination and improvisation.
Furthermore, trainers are given
important tips on proper warming
up and warming down. An index
helps readers to quickly locate
the required points of emphasis in
the context of the various training
games.

128 pages
Two-colour print
82 figures
Paperback, 14.8 x 21 cm
ISBN 1-84126-015-0
£ 12.95 UK/$ 17.95 US/
$ 25.95 CDN

**MEYER
& MEYER
SPORT**

MEYER & MEYER Verlag | Von-Coels-Straße 390 | D-52080 Aachen, Germany | Fax + + 49 (0)2 41 - 9 58 10-10

Technique & Tactics

Erich Kollath
**Soccer –
Technique & Tactics**

The essence of soccer is really the interplay between technique and tactics. In modern soccer these two components must complement each other. The author first deals intensively with soccer technique, extensively covering all movements with, without and around the ball. In the second part tactics are discussed, whereby the author differentiates between the individual tactics of the various playing positions, group tactics and team tactics. More than 150 drills and game patterns provide a diverse range of ideas for learning and improving soccer technique & tactics.

152 pages
83 photos, 28 illustrations
Paperback, 14.8 x 21 cm
ISBN 1-84126-016-9
£ 8.95 UK/$ 14.95 US/
$ 20.95 CDN